AF454329

Table Of Content

Table Of Content

Table Of Content

Table Of Content

Table Of Content

Table Of Content

Table Of Content

Table Of Content

Table Of
Content

Table Of Content

Table Of Content

Introducing

Embark on a transformative culinary odyssey with 'The Brazilian Organic Goodness,' a Vegan Cookbook that weaves together the rich tapestry of Brazil's vibrant cuisine and the myriad benefits of adopting a plant-based lifestyle. Beyond the tantalizing flavors that dance on your palate, each recipe embodies a commitment to environmental sustainability, ethical consumption, and personal well-being.

Indulge in the heartiness of feijoada, the zest of acai bowls, and the tropical medley of fruits, all while reaping the rewards of a vegan diet. Scientifically proven benefits, such as lower cholesterol, reduced risk of heart disease, and enhanced digestion, underscore the health advantages of plant-based living. Moreover, by choosing plant-centric meals, you contribute to a more sustainable future, reducing your ecological footprint and fostering a compassionate connection with the world around you.

'The Brazilian Organic Goodness' is not just a cookbook; it's an invitation to savor the symphony of flavors while embracing a lifestyle that nourishes your body, mind, and the planet. Join us in this culinary journey where every recipe reflects the fusion of taste, health, and ethical consciousness—a celebration of Brazil's diverse culture and the profound goodness of going vegan

SPECIAL SALAD

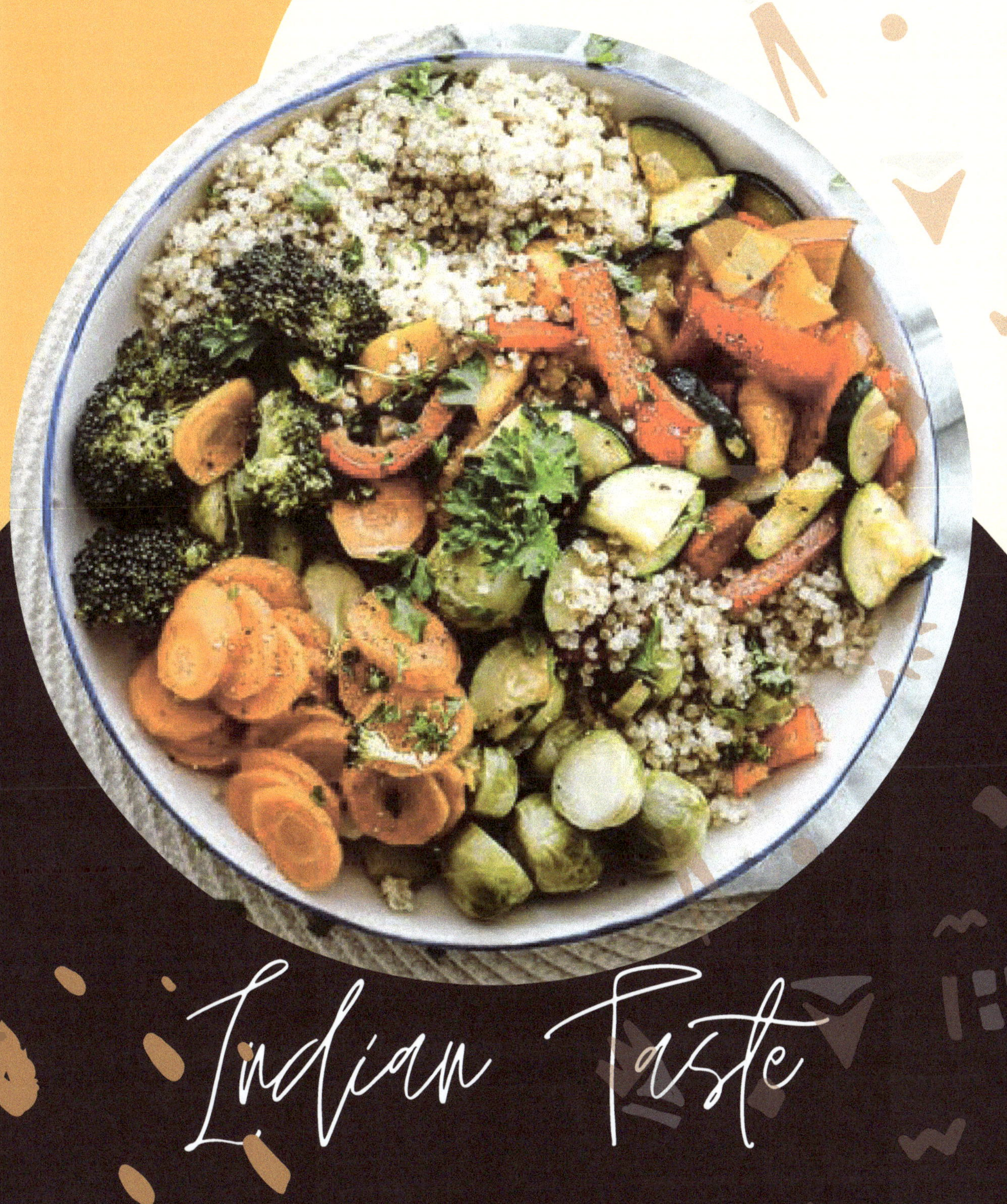

Special Salad Indian Taste

Ingredients

- 1 cup quinoa, rinsed
- 2 cups water
- 1 can (15 oz) chickpeas, drained and rinsed
- 1 cup cherry tomatoes, halved
- 1 cucumber, diced
- 1 red onion, finely chopped
- 1/2 cup fresh cilantro, chopped
- 1/4 cup fresh mint leaves, chopped

For dressing

- 3 tablespoons olive oil
- 2 tablespoons lemon juice
- 1 teaspoon ground cumin
- 1 teaspoon ground coriander
- 1/2 teaspoon turmeric
- 1/2 teaspoon garam masala
- Salt and pepper to taste

Instruction

1. Cook the Quinoa:
   - In a medium saucepan, combine quinoa and water. Bring to a boil, then reduce heat to low, cover, and simmer for 15-20 minutes or until quinoa is cooked and water is absorbed. Fluff quinoa with a fork and let it cool.
2. Prepare the Chickpeas:
   - In a separate pan, heat a bit of olive oil over medium heat. Add chickpeas and sauté for 5-7 minutes until they are slightly crispy. Set aside to cool.

 **Preparing** 15 Minutes

 **Cooking** 15 Minutes

 **Serving** 15 Minutes

Special Salad Indian Taste

Instruction

1. Make the Dressing:
   - In a small bowl, whisk together olive oil, lemon juice, cumin, coriander, turmeric, garam masala, salt, and pepper. Adjust the seasoning to taste.
2. Assemble the Salad:
   - In a large mixing bowl, combine cooked quinoa, sautéed chickpeas, cherry tomatoes, cucumber, red onion, cilantro, and mint.
3. Add the Dressing:
   - Pour the dressing over the salad and toss gently to coat all the ingredients evenly.
4. Chill and Serve:
   - Refrigerate the salad for at least 30 minutes to let the flavors meld. Serve chilled.

This vibrant and flavorful quinoa and chickpea salad captures the essence of Indian cuisine in a healthy and delicious way. Enjoy your Special Salad with an Indian twist!

Preparing
15 Minutes

Cooking
15 Minutes

Serving
15 Minutes

SPECIAL SALAD

Brazilian Hearts of Palm Salad

Ingredients

- 1 can (14 oz) hearts of palm, drained and sliced
- 1 cup cherry tomatoes, halved
- 1 avocado, diced
- 1/2 red onion, finely chopped
- 1/4 cup fresh cilantro, chopped
- 1/4 cup fresh parsley, chopped
- 1 jalapeño, seeds removed and finely chopped (optional for some heat)

For dressing

- 3 tablespoons olive oil
- 2 tablespoons lime juice
- 1 clove garlic, minced
- 1 teaspoon agave syrup or maple syrup
- Salt and pepper to taste
-

Instruction

1. Prepare the Hearts of Palm:
   - Drain the hearts of palm and slice them into bite-sized pieces.
2. Assemble the Salad:
   - In a large salad bowl, combine the hearts of palm, cherry tomatoes, diced avocado, red onion, cilantro, parsley, and jalapeño (if using).

Preparing
15 Minutes

Cooking
15 Minutes

Serving
15 Minutes

Brazilian Hearts of Palm Salad

Instruction

1. Make the Dressing:
   - In a small bowl, whisk together olive oil, lime juice, minced garlic, agave syrup, salt, and pepper.
2. Add the Dressing:
   - Pour the dressing over the salad and toss gently to coat all the ingredients evenly.
3. Chill and Serve:
   - Refrigerate the salad for about 15-30 minutes to allow the flavors to meld. Serve chilled.

This Brazilian Hearts of Palm Salad is a refreshing combination of textures and flavors. The hearts of palm provide a unique taste and pair wonderfully with the creamy avocado and zesty lime dressing. Enjoy your taste of Brazilian goodness!

Preparing
15 Minutes

Cooking
15 Minutes

Serving
15 Minutes

AMERICAN SALAD

best Choice

Southwest Quinoa Salad

Ingredients

- 1 cup quinoa, rinsed
- 2 cups water or vegetable broth
- 1 can (15 oz) black beans, drained and rinsed
- 1 cup corn kernels (fresh or thawed if using frozen)
- 1 cup cherry tomatoes, halved
- 1 bell pepper (any color), diced
- 1/2 red onion, finely chopped
- 1/4 cup fresh cilantro, chopped
- 1 avocado, diced

For dressing

- 3 tablespoons olive oil
- 2 tablespoons lime juice
- 1 clove garlic, minced
- 1 teaspoon ground cumin
- 1/2 teaspoon chili powder
- Salt and pepper to taste

Preparing
15 Minutes

Cooking
15 Minutes

Serving
15 Minutes

Southwest Quinoa Salad

Instruction

1. Cook the Quinoa:
   - In a medium saucepan, combine quinoa and water or vegetable broth. Bring to a boil, then reduce heat to low, cover, and simmer for 15-20 minutes or until quinoa is cooked and liquid is absorbed. Fluff quinoa with a fork and let it cool.
2. Assemble the Salad:
   - In a large salad bowl, combine cooked quinoa, black beans, corn, cherry tomatoes, bell pepper, red onion, cilantro, and diced avocado.

Southwest Quinoa Salad

Instruction

1. Make the Cilantro Lime Dressing:
2. In a small bowl, whisk together olive oil, lime juice, minced garlic, ground cumin, chili powder, salt, and pepper.
3. Add the Dressing:
4. Pour the cilantro lime dressing over the salad and toss gently to coat all the ingredients evenly.
5. Chill and Serve:
6. Refrigerate the salad for at least 30 minutes to let the flavors meld. Serve chilled.

This Southwest Quinoa Salad is packed with protein, fiber, and vibrant flavors, making it a wholesome and satisfying meal. Enjoy the taste of America with this delicious vegan salad!

Preparing
15 Minutes

Cooking
20 Minutes

Serving
15 Minutes

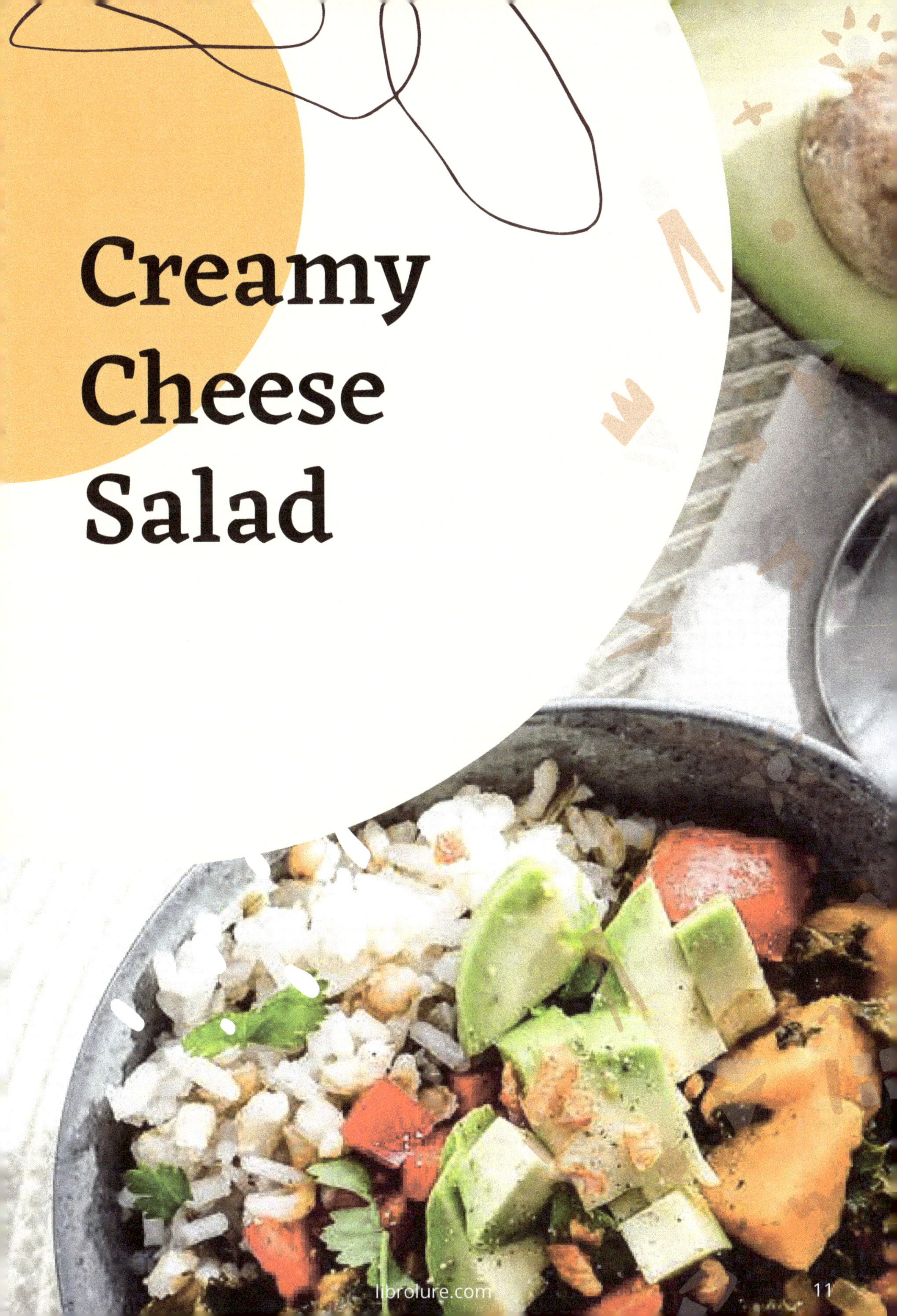

Creamy Cheese Salad

Vegan Creamy Cheese Salad

Ingredients

- 4 cups mixed salad greens (e.g., spinach, arugula, romaine)
- 1 cup cherry tomatoes, halved
- 1 cucumber, thinly sliced
- 1/2 red onion, thinly sliced
- 1 cup vegan cheese, cubed (choose your favorite variety)
- 1/4 cup sliced black olives

For dressing

- 1/2 cup raw cashews, soaked in hot water for 1 hour or overnight
- 1/4 cup nutritional yeast
- 2 tablespoons lemon juice
- 1 clove garlic, minced
- 1/2 teaspoon onion powder
- 1/2 teaspoon Dijon mustard
- 1/2 cup water (adjust for desired consistency)
- Salt and pepper to taste

Vegan Creamy Cheese Salad

Instruction

1. Prepare the Salad:
   - In a large salad bowl, combine the mixed salad greens, cherry tomatoes, cucumber, red onion, vegan cheese cubes, and black olives.
2. Make the Creamy Vegan Cheese Dressing:
   - Drain the soaked cashews and add them to a blender along with nutritional yeast, lemon juice, minced garlic, onion powder, Dijon mustard, and water.
   - Blend until smooth and creamy. Add more water if needed to achieve your desired dressing consistency. Season with salt and pepper to taste.
3. Dress the Salad:
   - Pour the creamy vegan cheese dressing over the salad ingredients.
4. Toss and Serve:
   - Gently toss the salad to coat all the ingredients with the creamy dressing.
5. Chill and Enjoy:
   - Refrigerate the salad for a short time if you prefer it chilled, or serve immediately.

QUINOA SALAD
100%
ORGANIC

Mango Avocado Quinoa Salad

Ingredients

- 1 cup quinoa, rinsed
- 2 cups water or vegetable broth
- 1 ripe mango, peeled, pitted, and diced
- 1 ripe avocado, peeled, pitted, and diced
- 1/2 cup red bell pepper, diced
- 1/4 cup red onion, finely chopped
- 1/4 cup fresh cilantro, chopped

For dressing

- 3 tablespoons olive oil
- 2 tablespoons lime juice
- 1 tablespoon maple syrup or agave nectar
- 1 teaspoon Dijon mustard
- Salt and pepper to taste
-

Instruction

1. Cook the Quinoa:
   - In a medium saucepan, combine quinoa and water or vegetable broth. Bring to a boil, then reduce heat to low, cover, and simmer for 15-20 minutes or until quinoa is cooked and liquid is absorbed. Fluff quinoa with a fork and let it cool.
2. Prepare the Salad Ingredients:
   - In a large salad bowl, combine the cooked quinoa, diced mango, diced avocado, red bell pepper, red onion, and chopped cilantro. If you're adding greens, toss them in as well.

Preparing
15 Minutes

Cooking
20 Minutes

Serving
15 Minutes

Mango Avocado Quinoa Salad

Instruction

1. Make the Lime Vinaigrette:
   - In a small bowl, whisk together olive oil, lime juice, maple syrup or agave nectar, Dijon mustard, salt, and pepper.
2. Dress the Salad:
   - Pour the lime vinaigrette over the salad ingredients and toss gently to coat.
3. Optional Toasted Seeds:
   - If desired, sprinkle toasted pumpkin seeds or sliced almonds on top for added crunch.
4. Chill and Serve:
   - Refrigerate the salad for at least 30 minutes before serving to allow the flavors to meld. Serve chilled.

This Mango Avocado Quinoa Salad is a refreshing and nutrient-packed dish with a delightful balance of sweetness, creaminess, and crunch. Enjoy this vibrant and flavorful vegan salad!

 **Preparing**
15 Minutes

 **Cooking**
15 Minutes

 **Serving**
15 Minutes

BREAKFAST AND BRUNCH

Best Choice

Indulge in the vibrant world of plant-based delights with our Vegan Breakfast and Brunch recipes. From wholesome quinoa bowls to luscious fruit-packed delights, discover the perfect start to your day—nourishing, cruelty-free, and bursting with flavors to elevate your mornings.

@librolure

Chickpea Scramble with Sweet Potato Hash

Ingredients

- 1 cup (150 g) cooked chickpeas, mashed
- ¼ cup (60 g) chopped onion
- ¼ cup (60 g) chopped bell pepper
- 2 tablespoons (30 ml) olive oil
- 1 teaspoon (5 g) smoked paprika
- Salt and pepper to taste
- 1 small sweet potato, diced

Instruction

1. In a large skillet, heat the olive oil over medium heat. Add the onion and bell pepper and cook until softened, about 5 minutes.
2. Add the mashed chickpeas, smoked paprika, salt, and pepper. Cook for 5 minutes more, breaking up the chickpeas with a fork.
3. Add the diced sweet potato and cook until tender, about 10 minutes more.
4. Serve warm with your favorite toppings, such as avocado, salsa, or hot sauce.

Preparing
15 Minutes

Cooking
20 Minutes

Vegan Avocado Toast with Smoked Paprika

Ingredients

- It is a long established
- fact that a reader will be
- distracted by the
- readable content of a page
- when looking at its layout
- The point of using Lorem Ipsum
- is that it has a more-or-less
- normal distribution of letters
- as opposed to using content
- here content here making it look
- like readable English

Instruction

It is a long established fact that a reader will be distracted by the readable content of a page when looking at its layout. The point of using Lorem Ipsum is that it has a more-or-less normal distribution of letters, as opposed to using 'Content here, content here', making it look like readable English.

Preparing
15 Minutes

Cooking
15 Minutes

Acai Bowl with Toppings

Ingredients

- 1 cup frozen acai berries
- 1 ripe banana
- 1/2 cup plant-based milk
- Toppings: Granola, sliced banana, coconut flakes, agave syrup

Instruction

1. In a blender, combine frozen acai berries, banana, and plant-based milk.
2. Blend until smooth and creamy.
3. Pour the acai mixture into a bowl.
4. Top with granola, sliced banana, coconut flakes, and a drizzle of agave syrup.
5. Enjoy this refreshing and nutritious Acai Bowl!

 **Preparing**
10 Minutes

 **Cooking**
0 Minutes

Tapioca Crepes with Vegan Cheese and Herbs

Ingredients

- 1 cup tapioca flour
- 1 cup water
- Pinch of salt
- Vegan cheese (shredded)
- Fresh herbs (cilantro or parsley, chopped)
- Diced tomatoes

Instruction

1. In a bowl, mix tapioca flour, water, and a pinch of salt until smooth.
2. Heat a non-stick pan over medium heat.
3. Pour the tapioca batter onto the pan to form a thin crepe.
4. Sprinkle vegan cheese, fresh herbs, and diced tomatoes on one half of the crepe.
5. Fold the crepe in half and cook until crispy on both sides.
6. Repeat for additional crepes.
7. Serve warm and enjoy these delicious Tapioca Crepes!

 **Preparing**
10 Minutes

 **Cooking**
5 Minutes

Brazilian-Style Black Bean and Plantain Stew

Ingredients

- 1 can black beans, drained and rinsed
- 2 ripe plantains, sliced
- 1 bell pepper, diced
- 1 onion, chopped
- 2 cloves garlic, minced
- 1 tsp cumin
- 1 tsp paprika
- Salt and pepper to taste
- Quinoa or rice for serving

Instruction

1. In a pot, sauté onion and garlic until softened.
2. Add bell pepper, plantains, black beans, cumin, paprika, salt, and pepper.
3. Stir well and let it simmer until plantains are tender.
4. Serve over quinoa or rice for a hearty Brazilian-Style Black Bean and Plantain Stew.

 **Preparing**
10 Minutes

 **Cooking**
10 Minutes

Cocada Overnight Oats

Ingredients

- 1 cup rolled oats
- 1 cup coconut milk
- 2 tbsp shredded coconut
- 1-2 tbsp maple syrup or agave syrup
- Sliced tropical fruits (mango, pineapple, passion fruit)

Instruction

1. In a jar, combine rolled oats, coconut milk, shredded coconut, and sweetener.
2. Stir well, cover, and refrigerate overnight.
3. In the morning, top with sliced mango, pineapple, and passion fruit.
4. Enjoy these Cocada Overnight Oats, a tropical delight!

 **Preparing**
12 hours

 **Cooking**
0 Minutes

Pão de Queijo (Vegan Cheese Bread)

Ingredients

- 2 cups tapioca flour
- 1 cup plant-based milk
- 1/2 cup vegetable oil
- 1 tsp salt
- 1 cup vegan cheese (shredded)

Instruction

1. Preheat the oven to 375°F (190°C) and grease a mini muffin tin.
2. In a saucepan, heat plant-based milk, vegetable oil, and salt until it begins to boil.
3. Remove from heat and slowly add tapioca flour, stirring constantly until well combined.
4. Let the mixture cool for a few minutes, then stir in the vegan cheese until smooth.
5. Spoon the batter into the mini muffin tin.
6. Bake for 15-20 minutes or until golden and puffed.
7. Allow to cool slightly before serving these delicious Vegan Pão de Queijo.

 **Preparing** 12 Minutes

 **Cooking** 20 Minutes

Vegan Main Dishes

Vegan Brazilian Feijoada

Vegan Black Bean Stew

Ingredients

- 2 cups black beans (canned or cooked)
- 1 large onion, chopped
- 3 cloves garlic, minced
- 1 cup carrots, diced
- 1 cup bell peppers, chopped
- 1 cup tomatoes, diced
- 1 bay leaf
- 1 tsp cumin
- 1 tsp paprika
- Salt and pepper to taste
- Chopped fresh cilantro for garnish

Instruction

1. In a large pot, sauté onions and garlic until softened.
2. Add carrots, bell peppers, tomatoes, and sauté for a few minutes.
3. Add black beans, bay leaf, cumin, paprika, salt, and pepper.
4. Simmer for 1-1.5 hours until flavors meld.
5. Garnish with fresh cilantro and serve over rice.

 **Preparing**
20 Minutes

 **Cooking**
70 Minutes

Hearts of Palm Moqueca

Ingredients

- 1 can hearts of palm, sliced
- 1 onion, sliced
- 2 bell peppers, sliced
- 2 tomatoes, diced
- 1 can coconut milk
- 2 tbsp olive oil
- 3 cloves garlic, minced
- 1 tsp paprika
- Salt and pepper to taste
- Fresh cilantro for garnish

Instruction

1. Sauté onions, garlic, and bell peppers in olive oil until softened.
2. Add tomatoes, hearts of palm, coconut milk, paprika, salt, and pepper.
3. Simmer for 20-25 minutes until vegetables are tender.
4. Garnish with fresh cilantro and serve over rice.

 **Preparing** 20 Minutes

 **Cooking** 25 Minutes

Mushroom Bobó

Ingredients

- 1 can hearts of palm, sliced
- 1 onion, sliced
- 2 bell peppers, sliced
- 2 tomatoes, diced
- 1 can coconut milk
- 2 tbsp olive oil
- 3 cloves garlic, minced
- 1 tsp paprika
- Salt and pepper to taste
- Fresh cilantro for garnish

Instruction

1. Sauté onions, garlic, and bell peppers in olive oil until softened.
2. Add tomatoes, hearts of palm, coconut milk, paprika, salt, and pepper.
3. Simmer for 20-25 minutes until vegetables are tender.
4. Garnish with fresh cilantro and serve over rice.

 **Preparing**
20 Minutes

 **Cooking**
30 Minutes

Jackfruit Shepherd's Pie

Ingredients

- 2 cans young jackfruit, shredded
- 1 onion, chopped
- 2 cloves garlic, minced
- 1 cup tomato sauce
- 1 cup vegetable broth
- 2 tbsp olive oil
- Mashed cassava (yuca)
- Salt and pepper to taste

Instruction

1. Sauté onions and garlic in olive oil until translucent.
2. Add shredded jackfruit, tomato sauce, and vegetable broth.
3. Simmer until jackfruit is tender.
4. In a baking dish, layer the jackfruit mixture and mashed cassava.
5. Bake until the top is golden brown.

 **Preparing** 30 Minutes

 **Cooking** 30 Minutes

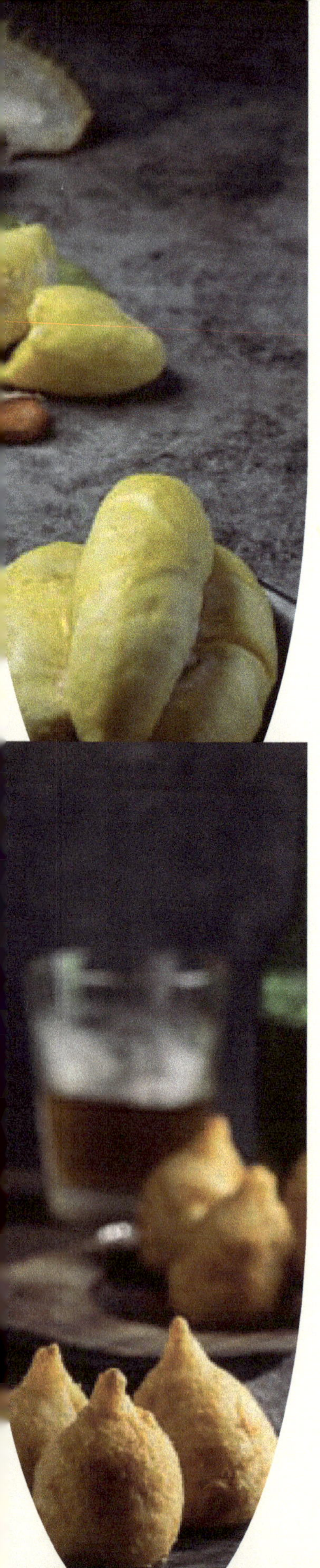

Jackfruit Coxinha

Ingredients

- 2 cans young jackfruit, shredded
- 1 onion, chopped
- 2 cloves garlic, minced
- 1 cup vegetable broth
- 2 cups cassava flour
- 2 cups water
- Salt and pepper to taste
- Vegetable oil for frying

Instruction

1. Sauté onions and garlic until softened.
2. Add shredded jackfruit and vegetable broth. Cook until jackfruit is tender.
3. In a separate pot, combine water, cassava flour, salt, and pepper to make a dough.
4. Take a portion of the dough, flatten it, and add a spoonful of jackfruit filling.
5. Shape into a drumstick, coat with more dough, and fry until golden brown.

 **Preparing**
45 Minutes

 **Cooking**
15 Minutes

Vegetable Vatapá

Ingredients

- 2 cups bread, cubed
- 1 cup coconut milk
- 1 cup peanuts, roasted
- 1 onion, chopped
- 2 cloves garlic, minced
- 1 cup tomatoes, diced
- 1 cup bell peppers, chopped
- 1 cup zucchini, diced
- 2 tbsp palm oil
- Salt and pepper to taste

Instruction

1. Soak bread in coconut milk until softened.
2. In a blender, combine soaked bread, peanuts, and blend into a smooth paste.
3. Sauté onions and garlic in palm oil until golden.
4. Add tomatoes, bell peppers, zucchini, and sauté until tender.
5. Stir in the peanut mixture, salt, and pepper. Simmer until thickened.

 **Preparing**
25 Minutes

 **Cooking**
40 Minutes

Vegan Baião de Dois

Ingredients

- 1 cup rice
- 1 cup black-eyed peas, cooked
- 1 cup coconut milk
- 1 onion, chopped
- 2 cloves garlic, minced
- 2 tbsp olive oil
- 1 cup collard greens, chopped
- Salt and pepper to taste

Instruction

1. Cook rice according to package instructions.
2. Sauté onions and garlic in olive oil until translucent.
3. Add black-eyed peas, coconut milk, collard greens, salt, and pepper.
4. Simmer until collard greens are wilted.
5. Serve over cooked rice.

Preparing
20 Minutes

Cooking
40 Minutes

Tutu de Feijão

Ingredients

- 2 cups black beans, cooked
- 1 cup cassava flour
- 1 onion, chopped
- 2 cloves garlic, minced
- 2 tbsp olive oil
- 1 tsp cumin
- Salt and pepper to taste

Instruction

1. In a blender, blend black beans into a smooth paste.
2. Sauté onions and garlic in olive oil until golden.
3. Add the bean paste, cassava flour, cumin, salt, and pepper.
4. Stir continuously until the mixture thickens.

 **Preparing**
15 Minutes

 **Cooking**
30 Minutes

Pumpkin Quibebe

Ingredients

- 4 cups pumpkin, diced
- 1 onion, chopped
- 2 cloves garlic, minced
- 2 tbsp olive oil
- 1 cup vegetable broth
- 1 tsp paprika
- Salt and pepper to taste

Instruction

1. Sauté onions and garlic in olive oil until softened.
2. Add diced pumpkin, vegetable broth, paprika, salt, and pepper.
3. Simmer until pumpkin is tender and the liquid has reduced.

Preparing
20 Minutes

Cooking
25 Minutes

Vegan Cuscuz Paulista

Ingredients

- 2 cups couscous
- 2 cups vegetable broth
- 2 tbsp olive oil
- 1 onion, finely chopped
- 2 cloves garlic, minced
- 1 bell pepper, diced
- 1 zucchini, diced
- 1 cup cherry tomatoes, halved
- 1 cup corn kernels (fresh or thawed if using frozen)
- 1/2 cup black olives, sliced
- 1/4 cup raisins (optional)
- Salt and pepper to taste
- Chopped fresh parsley for garnish

Instruction

In a bowl, combine couscous with vegetable broth. Let it sit for 10-15 minutes or until the couscous has absorbed the broth.

In a large pan, heat olive oil over medium heat. Add chopped onion and sauté until translucent. Add minced garlic and sauté for an additional 1-2 minutes.

Add diced bell pepper, zucchini, cherry tomatoes, corn, black olives, and raisins (if using). Sauté until the vegetables are tender.

Steam the cuscuz over medium heat for about 15-20 minutes or until it becomes firm. If you don't have a cuscuzera, you can use a regular steamer or improvise with a colander placed over a pot of simmering water.

 **Preparing**
15 Minutes

 **Cooking**
25 Minutes

Vegan Acarajé

Ingredients

- 2 cups black-eyed pea flour
- 1 cup water
- 1 tsp salt
- Vegetable oil for frying
- Vegan stuffing options: Vatapá, sliced tomatoes, shredded lettuce, hot peppers

Instruction

1. Mix black-eyed pea flour, water, and salt to form a thick batter.
2. Heat oil in a deep pan. Drop spoonfuls of batter into the oil, frying until golden.
3. Split each acarajé and stuff with vegan options. Serve warm.

 **Preparing** 15 Minutes   **Cooking** 25 Minutes

Vegan Picadinho

Ingredients

- 2 cups textured vegetable protein (TVP)
- 1 onion, chopped
- 2 cloves garlic, minced
- 2 tomatoes, diced
- 1 bell pepper, diced
- 1 cup black beans, cooked
- 1 tsp cumin
- 1 tsp paprika
- Salt and pepper to taste
- Chopped fresh cilantro for garnish

Instruction

1. Rehydrate TVP according to package instructions.
2. Sauté onions and garlic until golden. Add tomatoes, bell pepper, and cook until softened.
3. Add rehydrated TVP, black beans, cumin, paprika, salt, and pepper. Cook until well combined.
4. Garnish with fresh cilantro and serve over rice.

 **Preparing** 15 Minutes

 **Cooking** 25 Minutes

Vegan Xinxim de Soja

Ingredients

- 2 cups soy chunks, rehydrated
- 1 cup peanuts
- 1 onion, chopped
- 2 cloves garlic, minced
- 1 cup coconut milk
- 1 cup vegetable broth
-
- 1 bell pepper, sliced
- 1 tbsp palm oil
- 1 tsp ground ginger
- Salt and pepper to taste

Instruction

1. In a blender, grind peanuts into a paste.
2. Sauté onions and garlic in palm oil until translucent. Add bell pepper and cook until softened.
3. Add rehydrated soy chunks, peanut paste, coconut milk, vegetable broth, ginger, salt, and pepper.
4. Simmer until the sauce thickens. Serve over rice.

 **Preparing**
20 Minutes

Cooking
30 Minutes

Vegan Barreado

Ingredients

- 2 cups oyster mushrooms, shredded
- 1 onion, sliced
- 2 cloves garlic, minced
- 2 tomatoes, diced
- 1 cup vegetable broth
- 1 cup red wine
- 2 bay leaves
- 1 tsp cumin
- Salt and pepper to taste
- Sliced green onions for garnish

Instruction

1. Sauté onions and garlic until golden. Add shredded oyster mushrooms and cook until browned.
2. Add tomatoes, vegetable broth, red wine, bay leaves, cumin, salt, and pepper.
3. Simmer until the mushrooms are tender. Garnish with sliced green onions.

 **Preparing** 15 Minutes **Cooking** 30 Minutes

Vegan Baião de Dois com Jaca

Ingredients

- 1 cup rice
- 1 cup green jackfruit, shredded
- 1 cup black-eyed peas, cooked
- 1 cup coconut milk
- 1 onion, chopped
- 2 cloves garlic, minced
-
- 2 tbsp olive oil
- 1 cup collard greens, chopped
- Salt and pepper to taste

Instruction

1. Cook rice according to package instructions.
2. Sauté onions and garlic in olive oil until translucent. Add jackfruit and cook until tender.
3. Add cooked black-eyed peas, coconut milk, collard greens, salt, and pepper.
4. Simmer until collard greens are wilted. Serve over rice.

 **Preparing**
20 Minutes

 **Cooking**
40 Minutes

Vegan Bobó de Palmito

Ingredients

- 2 cans hearts of palm, sliced
- 1 onion, chopped
- 2 cloves garlic, minced
- 1 cup coconut milk
- 1 cup vegetable broth
- 2 tbsp red palm oil
- 1 bell pepper, sliced
- 1 tsp ground coriander
- Salt and pepper to taste

Instruction

1. Sauté onions and garlic in red palm oil until golden. Add bell pepper and cook until softened.
2. Add sliced hearts of palm, coconut milk, vegetable broth, ground coriander, salt, and pepper.
3. Simmer until the mixture thickens. Serve over rice.

 **Preparing** 25 Minutes

 **Cooking** 30 Minutes

Amazing Vegan
Brazilian recipes

Plantain Moqueca

Ingredients

- 3 ripe plantains, sliced
- 1 onion, sliced
- 2 bell peppers, sliced
- 1 can coconut milk
- 2 tomatoes, diced
- 3 cloves garlic, minced
- 1 tbsp palm oil
- 1 tsp smoked paprika
- Salt and pepper to taste
- Fresh cilantro for garnish

Instruction

1. Sauté onions and garlic in palm oil until translucent.
2. Add bell peppers, tomatoes, and sliced plantains.
3. Pour in coconut milk, add smoked paprika, salt, and pepper.
4. Simmer until plantains are tender. Garnish with fresh cilantro.

 **Preparing**
20 Minutes

 **Cooking**
30 Minutes

Vegan Caruru

Ingredients

- 2 cups okra, chopped
- 1 cup spinach, chopped
- 1 onion, chopped
- 2 cloves garlic, minced
- 1/2 cup peanuts, roasted and ground
- 2 tbsp palm oil
- 1 tsp ground coriander
- Salt and pepper to taste

Instruction

1. Sauté onions and garlic in palm oil until golden.
2. Add chopped okra and spinach, cooking until wilted.
3. Stir in ground peanuts, ground coriander, salt, and pepper.

Preparing
15 Minutes

Cooking
25 Minutes

Brazilian Hominy with Vegetables

Ingredients

- 1 cup hominy corn
- 1 zucchini, diced
- 1 carrot, diced
- 1 potato, diced
- 1 onion, chopped
- 2 cloves garlic, minced
- 1 cup vegetable broth
- 1 bay leaf
- 1 tsp cumin
- Salt and pepper to taste
- Chopped parsley for garnish

Instruction

1. Sauté onions and garlic until golden.
2. Add hominy corn, zucchini, carrot, potato, and vegetable broth.
3. Season with bay leaf, cumin, salt, and pepper.
4. Simmer until vegetables are tender. Garnish with chopped parsley.

 **Preparing**
20 Minutes

 **Cooking**
40 Minutes

Vegan Feijão Tropeiro

Ingredients

- 2 cups black beans, cooked
- 1 cup cassava flour
- 1 cup collard greens, finely chopped
- 1 onion, chopped
- 2 cloves garlic, minced
- 1/2 cup vegan sausage, diced
- 2 tbsp olive oil
- Salt and pepper to taste

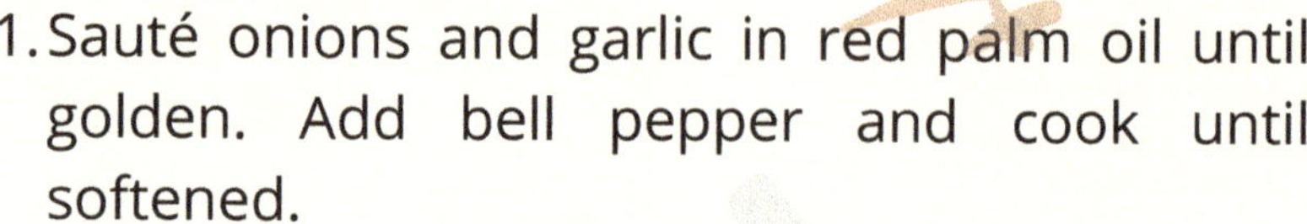

Instruction

1. Sauté onions and garlic in red palm oil until golden. Add bell pepper and cook until softened.
2. Add sliced hearts of palm, coconut milk, vegetable broth, ground coriander, salt, and pepper.
3. Simmer until the mixture thickens. Serve over rice.

Preparing
20 Minutes

Cooking
30 Minutes

Vegan Virado à Paulista

Ingredients

- 1 cup black-eyed peas, cooked
- 1 cup rice
- 1 cup collard greens, sliced
- 1 onion, chopped
- 2 cloves garlic, minced
- 2 tbsp olive oil
- Salt and pepper to taste

Instruction

1. Cook rice and black-eyed peas according to package instructions.
2. Sauté onions and garlic in olive oil until golden.
3. Add collard greens and cook until wilted. Season with salt and pepper.
4. Serve over rice and black-eyed peas.

 **Preparing**
15 Minutes

 **Cooking**
25 Minutes

Cassava Shepherd's Pie with Shitake

Ingredients

- 3 cups cassava, peeled and diced
- 1 cup coconut milk
- 2 tbsp vegan margarine
- 2 cups shitake mushrooms, sliced
- 1 onion, chopped
- 2 cloves garlic, minced
- 1 cup tomato sauce
- Salt and pepper to taste
- Chopped chives for garnish

Instruction

1. Boil cassava until tender. Mash with coconut milk and vegan margarine.
2. Sauté onions and garlic in olive oil until translucent.
3. Add shitake mushrooms, cooking until browned. Stir in tomato sauce.
4. In a baking dish, layer mashed cassava and shitake mixture. Bake until golden.
5. Garnish with chopped chives.

 **Preparing** 30 Minutes

 **Cooking** 30 Minutes

Vegan Dobradinha

Ingredients

- 2 cups jackfruit, boiled and shredded
- 1 cup black-eyed peas, cooked
- 1 cup rice
- 1 onion, chopped
- 2 cloves garlic, minced
- 2 tbsp olive oil
- 1 cup tomato sauce
- 1 tsp ground cumin
- Salt and pepper to taste

Instruction

1. Cook rice and black-eyed peas according to package instructions.
2. Sauté onions and garlic in olive oil until golden.

 **Preparing**
25 Minutes

 **Cooking**
35 Minutes

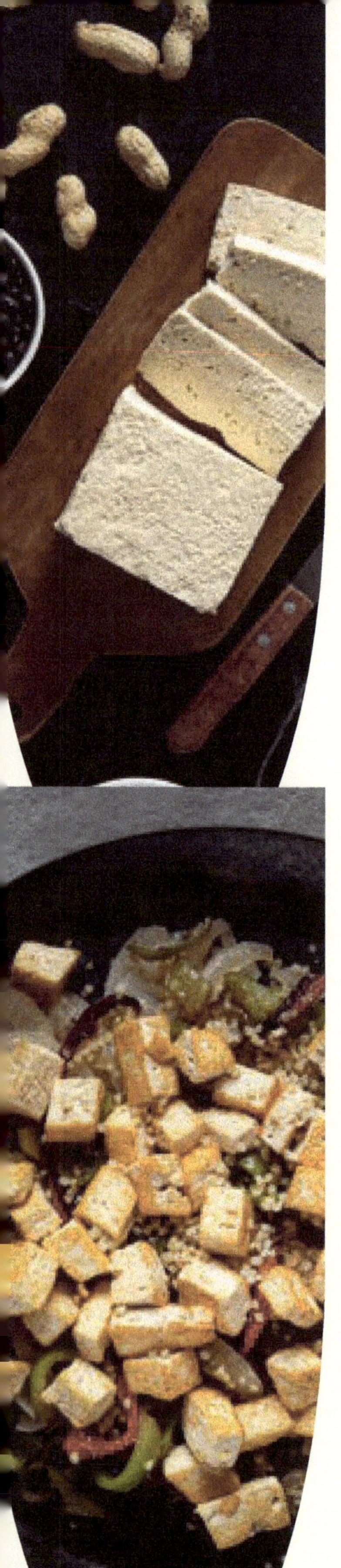

Vegan Tofu and Peanut Sauce

Ingredients

- 8 oz rice noodles, flat or thin
- 1 cup firm tofu, cubed
- 2 cups bean sprouts
- 1 cup carrots, julienned
- 1 red bell pepper, thinly sliced
- 3 green onions, sliced
- 1/4 cup peanuts, crushed
- Fresh cilantro for garnish
- Lime wedges for serving
- 1/4 cup smooth peanut butter
- 3 tbsp soy sauce
- 2 tbsp rice vinegar
- 1 tbsp maple syrup or agave nectar
- 1 clove garlic, minced
- 1 tsp grated ginger
- 1 tbsp sesame oil
- Sriracha or chili flakes to taste (optional)
- Water to adjust consistency

Instruction

Cook rice noodles

In a pan, sauté tofu cubes

In a bowl, whisk together peanut butter, soy sauce, rice vinegar, maple syrup, minced garlic, grated ginger, sesame oil, and Sriracha (if using). Add water gradually to achieve desired consistency.

In a large pan or wok, stir-fry julienned carrots, sliced bell pepper, and green onions until slightly tender

Squeeze lime over your serving, and enjoy this flavorful and satisfying Vegan Pad Thai with Tofu and Peanut Sauce

 **Preparing** 25 Minutes

 **Cooking** 30 Minutes

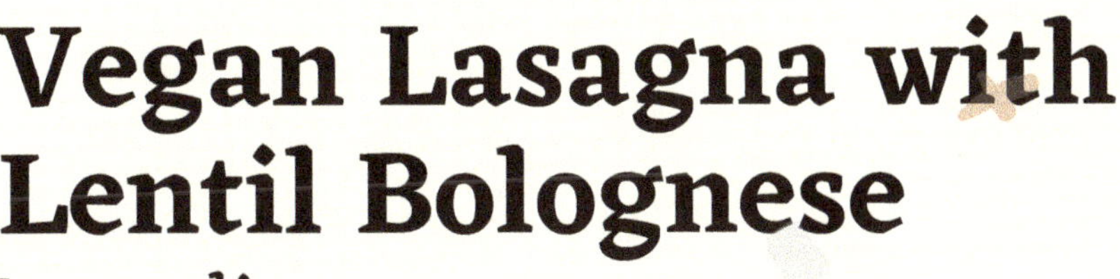

Vegan Lasagna with Lentil Bolognese

Ingredients

- 1 (14-ounce) can lentils, drained and rinsed
- 1 tablespoon olive oil
- 1 onion, chopped
- 2 carrots, chopped
- 2 celery stalks, chopped
- 4 cloves garlic, minced
- 1 (28-ounce) can crushed tomatoes
- 1 (15-ounce) can tomato sauce
- 1 teaspoon dried oregano
- 1 teaspoon dried basil
- 1 pound (450 g) dried lasagna noodles
- 1 (12-ounce) package vegan ricotta cheese
- 1 cup (240 ml) unsweetened soy milk
- 1/4 cup (60 ml) vegan parmesan cheese, optional
- Salt and pepper to taste

Instruction For the lentil bolognese

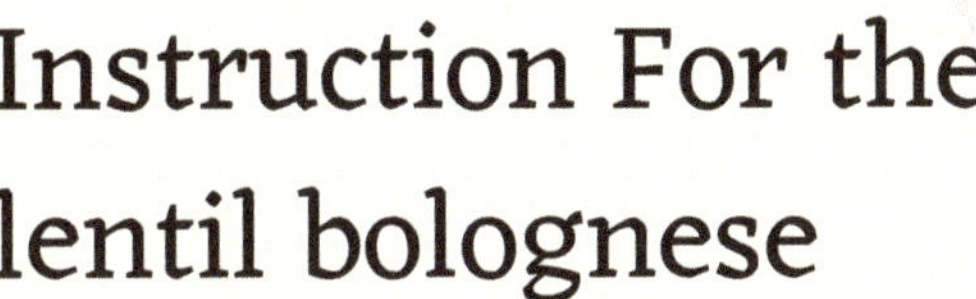

1. Heat the olive oil in a large saucepan over medium heat.
2. Add the onion, carrots, and celery and cook until softened, about 5 minutes.
3. Add the garlic and cook for 30 seconds more, until fragrant.
4. Stir in the lentils, crushed tomatoes, tomato sauce, oregano, basil, salt, and pepper.
5. Bring to a simmer and cook for 20 minutes, or until the sauce has thickened

Vegan Lasagna with Lentil Bolognese

Instruction For the lasagna

1. Preheat oven to 375°F (190°C).
2. Cook the lasagna noodles according to package directions.
3. In a medium bowl, combine the vegan ricotta cheese, soy milk, vegan parmesan cheese (if using), salt, and pepper.
4. To assemble the lasagna, spread a thin layer of béchamel sauce in the bottom of a 9x13-inch baking dish.
5. Top with a layer of lasagna noodles.
6. Spread a layer of lentil bolognese over the noodles.
7. Top with a layer of vegan ricotta cheese mixture.
8. Repeat layers of noodles, bolognese, and vegan ricotta cheese mixture until all of the ingredients are used.
9. Top with the remaining béchamel sauce.
10. Bake for 30-35 minutes, or until the lasagna is heated through and the béchamel sauce is bubbly.
11. Let stand for 10 minutes before serving.

 **Preparing**
25 Minutes

 **Cooking**
90 Minutes

Vegan Sushi with Avocado and Edamame

Ingredients

- 2 cups (500 g) cooked sushi rice, cooled
- 1 ripe avocado, sliced
- 1 cup (150 g) edamame, cooked and shelled
- 1 teaspoon wasabi paste
- 2 tablespoons vegan sushi vinegar
- Nori sheets
- Salt and pepper to taste

Instruction

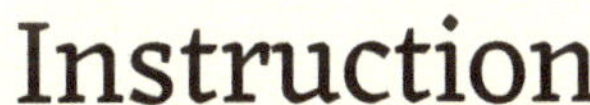

1. In a medium bowl, combine the sushi rice, avocado, edamame, wasabi paste, and vegan sushi vinegar.
2. Mix gently until the avocado and edamame are evenly distributed.
3. Season with salt and pepper to taste.
4. Spread a thin layer of rice mixture on a sheet of nori.
5. Fold the sides of the nori over the rice mixture, then roll the sushi tightly.
6. Repeat with the remaining nori and rice mixture.
7. Cut the sushi rolls into bite-sized pieces.
8. Serve immediately with your favorite toppings, such as soy sauce, pickled ginger, and wasabi.

Preparing
15 Minutes

Cooking
20 Minutes

Side Dishes

Vegan Mashed Potatoes with Tahini and Garlic

Ingredients

- 2 pounds (900 g) russet potatoes, peeled and cut into 1-inch cubes
- 2 cups (480 ml) vegetable broth
- 1/2 cup (120 ml) tahini
- 3 cloves garlic, minced
- 1/4 cup (60 ml) olive oil
- Salt and pepper to taste

Instruction

1. Place the potatoes in a large pot and cover with water.
2. Bring to a boil, then reduce heat and simmer for 15-20 minutes, or until the potatoes are tender.
3. Drain the potatoes and return them to the pot.
4. Using a potato masher or ricer, mash the potatoes until smooth.
5. Stir in the tahini, garlic, olive oil, salt, and pepper.
6. Taste and adjust seasonings as needed.
7. Serve immediately.

Preparing
15 Minutes

Cooking
30 Minutes

Roasted Vegetables with Herbs and Spices

Ingredients

- 1 pound (450 g) mixed vegetables, such as broccoli, carrots, zucchini, bell peppers, and onions
- 2 tablespoons olive oil
- 1 teaspoon paprika
- 1/2 teaspoon salt
- 1/4 teaspoon black pepper
- 1 tablespoon dried oregano

Instruction

1. Preheat oven to 400°F (200°C).
2. Toss the vegetables with olive oil, oregano, paprika, salt, and pepper.
3. Spread the vegetables on a baking sheet in a single layer.
4. Roast for 20-25 minutes, or until tender and slightly caramelized.

Preparing
10 Minutes

Cooking
35 Minutes

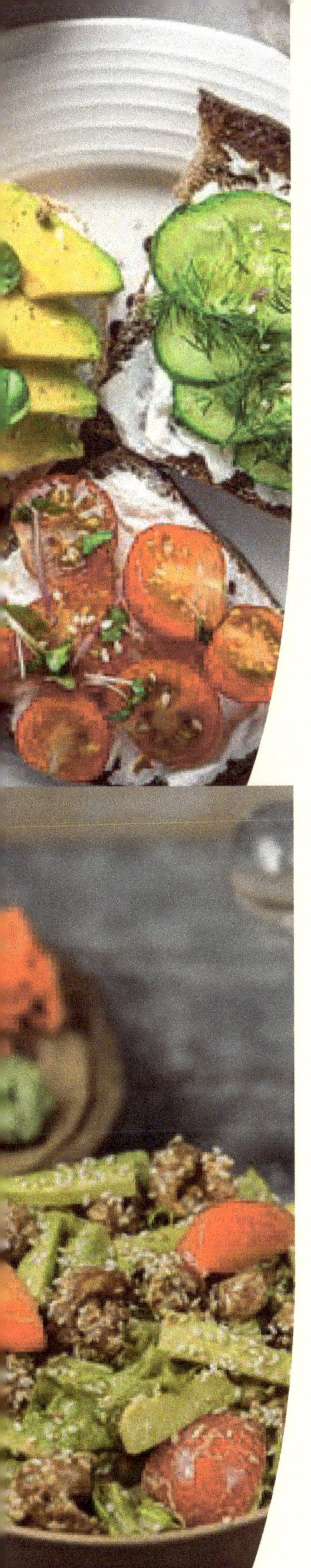

Vegan Salad with Quinoa, Chickpeas, and Avocado

Ingredients

- 1 cup (180 g) quinoa, cooked
- 1 (15-ounce) can chickpeas, drained and rinsed
- 1 ripe avocado, diced
- 1/2 cup (75 g) cherry tomatoes, halved
- 1/2 teaspoon black pepper
- 1/4 cup (30 g) chopped red onion
- 1/4 cup (30 g) chopped fresh cilantro
- 1/4 cup (60 ml) olive oil
- 1 tablespoon lemon juice
- 1 teaspoon salt

Instruction

1. Combine the quinoa, chickpeas, avocado, cherry tomatoes, red onion, and cilantro in a large bowl.
2. In a small bowl, whisk together the olive oil, lemon juice, salt, and pepper.
3. Pour the dressing over the salad and toss to coat.

 **Preparing**
15 Minutes

Cooking
10 Minutes

Vegan Pasta Salad with Sun-Dried Tomatoes and Basil

Ingredients

- 1/4 cup (60 ml) extra virgin olive oil
- 2 tablespoons lemon juice
- 1 tablespoon Dijon mustard
- 1 tablespoon chopped fresh basil
- 1/2 teaspoon salt
- 1/4 teaspoon black pepper

For salad

- 1 pound (450 g) cooked pasta, such as penne or fusilli
- 1/2 cup (75 g) sun-dried tomatoes, chopped
- 1/4 cup (30 g) pine nuts
- 1/4 cup (30 g) chopped fresh basil
- 1/4 cup (60 ml) vegan Parmesan cheese (optional)

Instruction

1. In a small bowl, whisk together the olive oil, lemon juice, Dijon mustard, basil, salt, and pepper.
2. For the salad:
3.
4. Combine the cooked pasta, sun-dried tomatoes, pine nuts, basil, and vegan Parmesan cheese (if using) in a large bowl.
5. Pour in the dressing and toss to coat.

 **Preparing**
15 Minutes

Cooking
10 Minutes

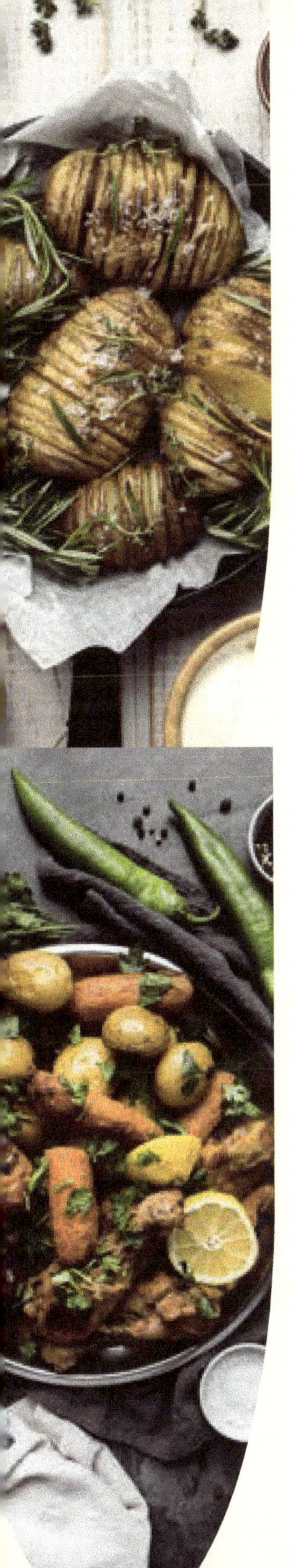

Vegan Roasted Potatoes with Rosemary and Thyme

Ingredients

- 2 pounds (900 g) russet potatoes, peeled and quartered
- 2 tablespoons olive oil
- 1 tablespoon chopped fresh rosemary
- 1 tablespoon chopped fresh thyme
- 1/2 teaspoon salt
- 1/4 teaspoon black pepper

Instruction

1. Preheat oven to 400°F (200°C).
2. In a large bowl, toss the potatoes with olive oil, rosemary, thyme, salt, and pepper.
3. Spread the potatoes on a baking sheet in a single layer.
4. Roast for 20-25 minutes, or until the potatoes are tender and slightly crispy.

 **Preparing**
15 Minutes

 **Cooking**
25 Minutes

Vegan Lentil Salad with Lemon and Dill

Ingredients

- 1 cup (190 g) green or brown lentils, cooked
- 1/2 cup (75 g) chopped red onion
- 1/4 cup (30 g) chopped fresh dill
- 1/4 cup (60 ml) olive oil
- 2 tablespoons lemon juice
- 1 teaspoon salt
- 1/2 teaspoon black pepper

Instruction

1. In a large bowl, combine the cooked lentils, red onion, and dill.
2. For the dressing:
3.
4. In a small bowl, whisk together the olive oil, lemon juice, salt, and pepper.
5. Pour the dressing over the lentils and toss to coat.

 **Preparing** 15 Minutes

 **Cooking** 15 Minutes

Vegan Black Bean Burgers

Ingredients

- 1 (15-ounce) can black beans, drained and rinsed
- 1/2 cup (75 g) rolled oats
- 1/4 cup (30 g) bread crumbs
- 1/4 cup (60 ml) olive oil
- 2 tablespoons soy sauce
- 1 tablespoon lime juice
- 1 teaspoon chili powder
- 1/2 teaspoon cumin
- 1/4 teaspoon salt
- 1/4 teaspoon black pepper
- 1/2 cup (75 g) shredded cabbage
- 1/4 cup (60 ml) vegan mayonnaise
- 1 tablespoon lime juice
- 1/2 teaspoon salt
- 1/4 teaspoon black pepper

Instruction

1. In a food processor, combine the black beans, oats, breadcrumbs, olive oil, soy sauce, lime juice, chili powder, cumin, salt, and pepper.
2. Process until the mixture is well combined and forms a chunky paste.
3. Form the mixture into 4 patties.
4. Heat a large skillet over medium heat.

Cook the patties for 5-7 minutes per side, or until golden brown and heated through.

 **Preparing** 15 Minutes    **Cooking** 15 Minutes

Vegan Falafel

Ingredients

- 1 (15-ounce) can chickpeas, drained and rinsed
- ¼ cup (60 ml) olive oil
- ¼ cup (60 ml) water
- 2 tablespoons lemon juice
- 2 tablespoons tahini paste
- 1 tablespoon ground cumin
- 1 teaspoon ground coriander
- ½ teaspoon salt
- ¼ teaspoon black pepper
- ¼ cup (30 g) chopped fresh cilantro
- 1 cup (80 g) all-purpose flour
- Vegetable oil for frying (or optional air fryer)

Instruction

1. In a food processor, combine the chickpeas, olive oil, water, lemon juice, tahini, cumin, coriander, salt, and pepper.
2. Process until the mixture is well combined and forms a chunky paste.
3. Add the cilantro and pulse a few times to incorporate.
4. Add the all-purpose flour and pulse until the mixture is just combined.
5. Form the mixture into 12-15 balls.
6. Heat the vegetable oil in a large skillet over medium-high heat.

Fry the falafel balls in batches for 2-3 minutes per side, or until golden brown and heated through.

 **Preparing**
15 Minutes

 **Cooking**
15 Minutes

Vegan Buffalo Cauliflower Bites

Ingredients

- 1 head (1 pound) cauliflower, cut into bite-sized florets
- 1/4 cup (60 ml) olive oil
- 1/2 cup (75 g) all-purpose flour
- 1 teaspoon salt
- 1/2 teaspoon black pepper
- 1/2 cup (120 ml) vegan buffalo sauce
- 1/4 cup (30 g) vegan cheese shreds (optional)

Instruction

1. Preheat oven to 400°F (200°C).
2. In a large bowl, toss the cauliflower florets with olive oil, flour, salt, and pepper until evenly coated.
3. Spread the cauliflower florets in a single layer on a baking sheet.
4. Roast for 20-25 minutes, or until tender and golden brown.
5. While the cauliflower is roasting, prepare the buffalo sauce. In a small saucepan, heat the vegan buffalo sauce over medium heat.
6. Once the cauliflower is roasted, pour the buffalo sauce over the florets and toss to coat.
7. If using the vegan cheese shreds, sprinkle them over the cauliflower bites and return to the oven for 2-3 minutes, or until the cheese is melted and bubbly.

 **Preparing**
15 Minutes

 **Cooking**
25 Minutes

Delicious

VEGAN DESSERTS

Vegan Brownies

Ingredients

- 1 cup (120 g) all-purpose flour
- 1 teaspoon baking powder
- 1/2 teaspoon salt
- 1 (15-ounce) can sweetened condensed coconut milk
- 1 (13.5-ounce) can black beans, drained and rinsed
- 1/2 cup (75 g) unsweetened cocoa powder
- 1/2 cup (100 g) granulated sugar
- 1/4 cup (60 ml) plant-based milk
- 1 teaspoon vanilla extract
- 1/4 teaspoon instant espresso powder (optional)

Instruction

1. Preheat oven to 350°F (175°C). Grease an 8x8-inch baking pan with vegan butter.
2. In a medium bowl, whisk together the flour, baking powder, and salt.
3. In a large bowl, combine the sweetened condensed coconut milk, black beans, cocoa powder, granulated sugar, plant-based milk, vanilla extract, and espresso powder (if using).
4. Pour the wet ingredients into the dry ingredients and whisk until just combined.
5. Pour the batter into the prepared baking pan and smooth the top with a spatula.
6. Sprinkle with chocolate chips (if using).
7. Bake for 30-35 minutes, or until a toothpick inserted into the center comes out with a few moist crumbs.

 **Preparing**
15 Minutes

 **Cooking**
35 Minutes

Vegan Chocolate Avocado Mousse

Ingredients

- 2 ripe avocados, pitted and peeled
- 1/2 cup (120 ml) unsweetened cocoa powder
- 1/4 cup (60 ml) maple syrup
- 1 teaspoon vanilla extract
- 1/4 teaspoon salt

Instruction

1. In a food processor, combine the avocados, cocoa powder, maple syrup, vanilla extract, and salt.
2. Process until smooth and creamy.
3. Taste and adjust sweetness and saltiness to your liking.
4. Pour the mousse into individual serving glasses or bowls.
5. Chill for at least 2 hours, or overnight, to allow the mousse to set.
6. Garnish with chocolate shavings or fresh berries, if desired.

Preparing
120 Minutes

Cooking
15 Minutes

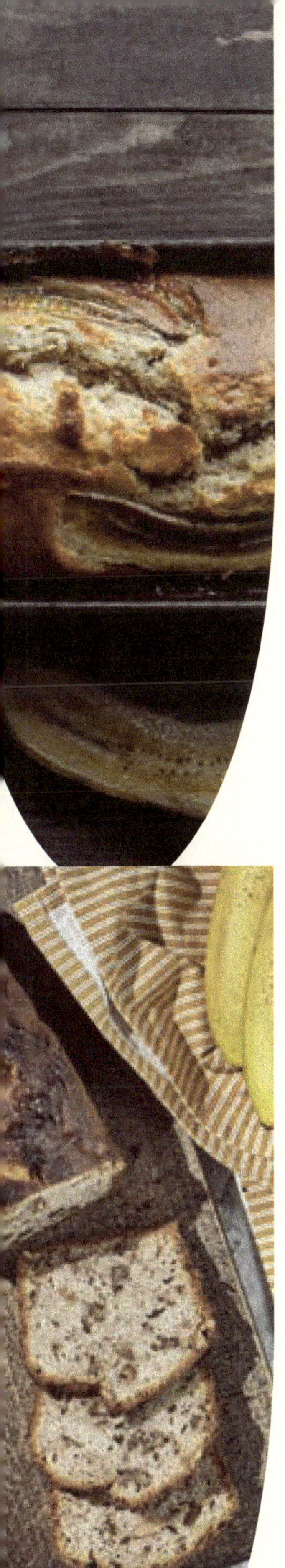

Vegan Banana Bread

Ingredients

- 3 ripe bananas, mashed
- 1 cup (225 g) granulated sugar
- 1/2 cup (120 ml) unsweetened soy milk
- 1 teaspoon vanilla extract
- 1/2 cup (1 stick) vegan butter, melted
- 2 cups (240 g) all-purpose flour
- 1 teaspoon baking soda
- 1/2 teaspoon salt
- 1/2 cup (75 g) chopped walnuts (optional)
- For the streusel topping (optional):
-
- 1/2 cup (60 g) all-purpose flour
- 1/4 cup (60 ml) light brown sugar
- 1/4 cup (60 ml) vegan butter, cold and cubed

Instruction

1. Preheat oven to 350°F (175°C). Grease an 8x8-inch baking pan.
2. In a large bowl, combine the mashed bananas, granulated sugar, soy milk, vanilla extract, and vegan butter.
3. In a separate bowl, whisk together the flour, baking soda, and salt.
4. Gradually add the dry ingredients to the wet ingredients, mixing until just combined.
5. If using walnuts, stir them into the batter.
6. Pour the batter into the prepared baking pan.

 **Preparing** 15 Minutes

 **Cooking** 30 Minutes

Vegan Ice Cream

Ingredients

- 2 cups (480 ml) full-fat coconut milk
- 1 cup (200 g) granulated sugar
- 1/2 cup (120 ml) plant-based milk
- 1 tablespoon vanilla extract
- 1/4 teaspoon salt
- 1/2 cup (75 g) chopped chocolate chips
- 1/4 cup (30 g) vegan chocolate syrup
- 1/4 cup (30 g) chopped nuts
- 1/4 cup (30 g) dried fruit

Instruction

1. In a medium saucepan, combine the coconut milk, sugar, plant-based milk, vanilla extract, and salt.
2. Bring to a simmer over medium heat, whisking constantly until the sugar is dissolved.
3. Remove from heat and let cool completely.
4. Pour the cooled mixture into a blender and blend until smooth.
5. Pour the mixture into an airtight container and freeze for at least 4 hours, or overnight.
6. After 4 hours, remove the ice cream from the freezer and let it soften for a few minutes.
7. Using a fork or an ice cream scoop, churn the ice cream until it is smooth and creamy.
8. Add the desired flavorings and churn again until evenly distributed.

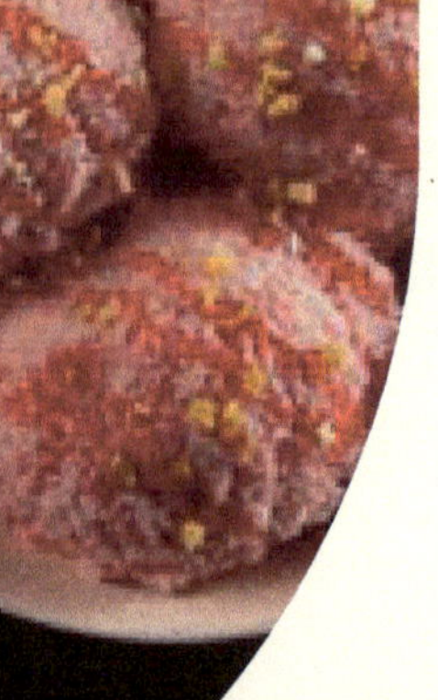

 **Preparing**
4 Hours

 **Cooking**
0 Minutes

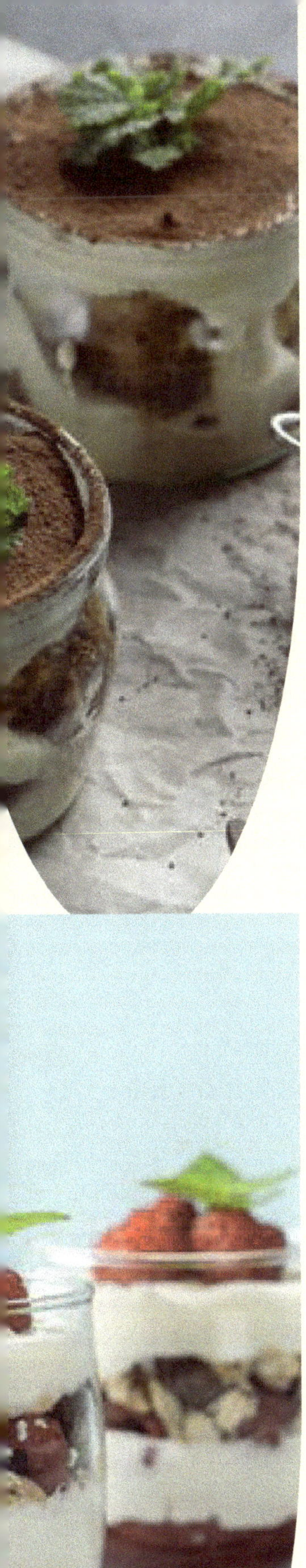

Vegan Panna Cotta

Ingredients

- 1 cup (240 ml) plant-based milk (such as soy, almond, or oat milk)
- 1 cup (200 g) granulated sugar
- 2 tablespoons cornstarch
- 1 teaspoon vanilla extract
- 1 teaspoon agar-agar powder (or 1 tablespoon unflavored gelatin)
- Fresh berries

Instruction

1. In a medium saucepan, whisk together the plant-based milk, sugar, cornstarch, and vanilla extract.
2. Bring to a simmer over medium heat, whisking constantly until the sugar is dissolved and the mixture thickens.
3. Remove from heat and stir in the agar-agar powder or gelatin.
4. Let cool slightly.
5. Pour the mixture into serving glasses or ramekins.
6. Refrigerate for at least 4 hours, or overnight, to allow the panna cotta to set.

 **Preparing**
4 Hours

 **Cooking**
0 Minutes

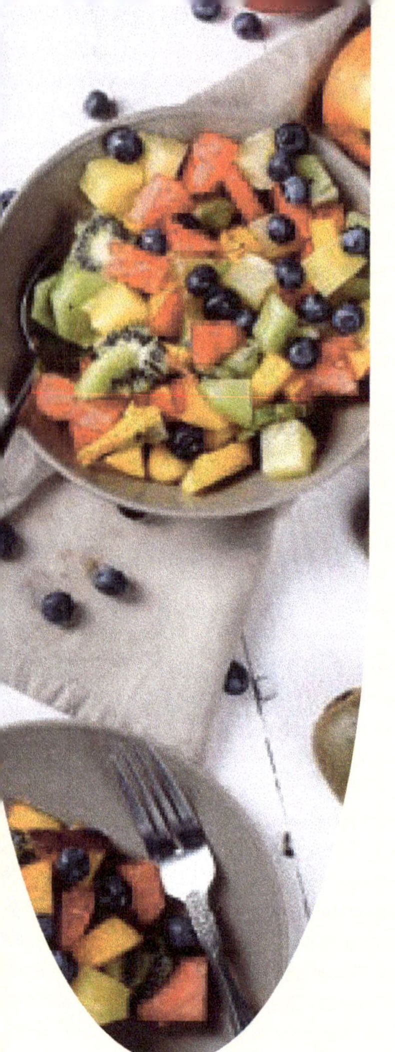

Vegan Fruit Salad with Balsamic Glaze

Ingredients

- 2 cups (300 g) mixed fresh berries (strawberries, blueberries, raspberries)
- 1 cup (150 g) chopped cantaloupe or honeydew melon
- 1/2 cup (75 g) chopped grapes
- 1/4 cup (60 ml) vegan honey or maple syrup
- 1/4 cup (60 ml) balsamic vinegar
- 1 tablespoon vegan honey or maple syrup
- 1/4 teaspoon ground cinnamon
- 1 tablespoon lemon juice
- 1/2 teaspoon ground cinnamon

Instruction

1. In a large bowl, combine the berries, melon, and grapes.
2. In a small bowl, whisk together the vegan honey, lemon juice, and cinnamon.
3. Pour the dressing over the fruit salad and toss to coat.
4. Let the salad sit for 10 minutes to allow the flavors to meld.
5. For the balsamic glaze:
6.
7. In a small saucepan, heat the balsamic vinegar over medium heat until it is reduced to a syrupy consistency, about 5-7 minutes.
8. Stir in the vegan honey and cinnamon.
9. Let the glaze cool slightly.

 **Preparing** 10 Minutes

Cooking 7 Minutes

Vegan Açaí Bowl

Ingredients

- 2 frozen açaí packs
- 1 ripe banana
- 1/2 cup mixed berries
- 1/4 cup granola
- 1 tbsp agave syrup
- Coconut flakes for garnish

Instruction

1. Blend açaí packs, banana, and berries until smooth.
2. Pour into a bowl, top with granola, drizzle with agave syrup, and garnish with coconut flakes.

 **Preparing**
10 Minutes

Cooking
0 Minutes

Vegan Cocada

Ingredients

- 2 cups shredded coconut
- 1 cup coconut milk
- 1 cup sugar
- 1/4 cup water
- 1/4 cup vegan margarine
- A pinch of salt

Instruction

1. n a pot, combine coconut, coconut milk, sugar, water, margarine, and salt.
2. Cook over medium heat, stirring, until the mixture thickens and turns golden.
3. Drop spoonfuls onto a parchment-lined tray and let cool.

 **Preparing**
10 Minutes

 **Cooking**
15 Minutes

Vegan Passion Fruit Mousse

Ingredients

- 1 cup passion fruit pulp
- 1 cup coconut cream
- 1/2 cup sugar
- 2 tbsp cornstarch
- Vegan whipped cream for topping

Instruction

1. In a saucepan, mix passion fruit pulp, coconut cream, sugar, and cornstarch.
2. Cook over medium heat until thickened. Let it cool.
3. Spoon into serving glasses and refrigerate. Top with vegan whipped cream before serving.

 **Preparing**
15 Minutes

 **Cooking**
10 Minutes

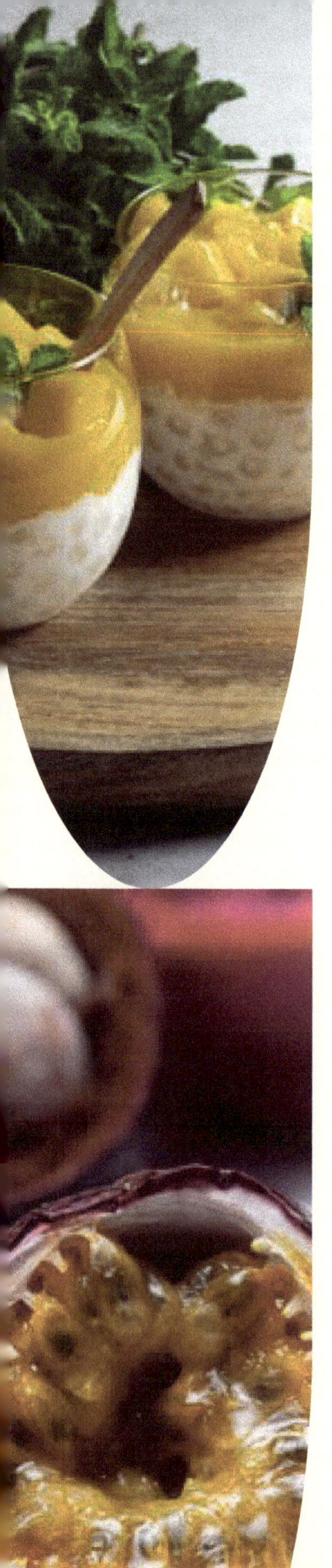

Vegan Paçoca Ice Cream

Ingredients

- 2 cups peanuts, roasted
- 1 cup coconut milk
- 1/2 cup sugar
- 1 tsp vanilla extract
- Pinch of salt

Instruction

1. In a blender, blend peanuts until crumbly.
2. Add coconut milk, sugar, vanilla extract, and salt. Blend until smooth.
3. Pour into an ice cream maker and churn according to the manufacturer's instructions.

 **Preparing**
10 Minutes

 **Cooking**
0 Minutes

Vegan Coconut Truffles

Ingredients

- 2 cups shredded coconut
- 1 cup coconut condensed milk
- Vegan chocolate for coating
- Vegan sprinkles for decoration

Instruction

1. In a pan, combine shredded coconut and coconut condensed milk.
2. Cook over low heat until the mixture thickens. Let it cool.
3. Shape into small balls, dip in melted chocolate, and sprinkle with vegan sprinkles.

 **Preparing**
15 Minutes

 **Cooking**
10 Minutes

Chef Dilson Mesquita

Embarking on the journey of a vegan cookbook not only celebrates culinary creativity but also champions a holistic approach to well-being. Crafting recipes centered around plant-based goodness is an invitation to a world of health benefits.

Abundant in nutrient-dense fruits, vibrant vegetables, and wholesome grains, the recipes promise not just delicious flavors but also a pathway to enhanced heart health and a reduced risk of chronic ailments. Through the pages of this cookbook, discover the transformative power of plant-based living—elevating energy levels, fortifying the immune system, and achieving a harmonious balance in both body and mind.

The culinary creations herein not only tantalize taste buds but also align with ethical considerations, promoting animal welfare and environmental sustainability. Each dish becomes a conscious choice towards a healthier self, a compassionate existence, and a sustainable culinary legacy for generations to come. Welcome to a culinary exploration that transcends the ordinary, embracing the art of vegan cooking as a pathway to a vibrant and purposeful life.